OPEN ENDED STORIES

Milton Velder
Edwin Cohen

Ernst Klett Schulbuchverlag
Stuttgart Düsseldorf Berlin Leipzig

Gedruckt auf Eural PRO
hergestellt von Papeterie du Bourray
aus 100 % Altpapier.

1. Auflage 1 16 15 14 13 12 | 1998 97 96 95 94

Alle Drucke dieser Auflage können im Unterricht nebeneinander benutzt werden; sie sind untereinander unverändert. Die letzte Zahl bezeichnet das Jahr dieses Druckes.

Zeichnungen: Ned Glattauer. Umschlaggestaltung: Hans Lämmle, Stuttgart.
Druck: Wilhelm Röck, Weinsberg. Printed in Germany.
ISBN 3-12-547500-7

Contents

Open-Ended Stories

All the stories in this book are 'open-ended': in other words it is up to you, the reader, to decide how a particular story could or should end. These stories are set in America (you will notice the American spelling), but they deal with problems which young people almost anywhere could be faced with.

In the *Annotations*, at the end of each story, difficult words are defined in easy terms, and colloquial, slang or purely American expressions are explained.

The *Questions on the story* are intended to help you understand the story fully, by focussing your attention on particular details or events.

In the section *What happens now?* you are asked questions aimed at stimulating discussion and which will help you to make up your mind how the story should end. Finally, you are asked to complete the story in your own words.

Remember that there is no 'right' or 'wrong' ending to any of the stories. You must decide: what happens now?

Mind Your Own Business

Bill was puzzled. That was the second time today Stan had walked by without saying hello. "Did I do anything wrong?" he kept asking himself.

He was even beginning to worry a little. After all, the young men had been buddies since first grade. Now they were in high school. They had been through a lot together.

The bell snapped Bill from his thoughts. He hurried along. Stan would be in his next class. Maybe if Bill cornered him at the close of the period he would explain his strange behavior.

When Bill reached his desk the class had already begun. He looked over at Stan. Suddenly he was startled to find that his friend's eyes were hidden behind a pair of dark glasses. Now Bill couldn't take his eyes off him.

Stan usually helped to make social studies discussion come alive. Today he slumped in his chair, completely tuned out. From time to time, his cheek would twitch. Just before the bell rang, Bill was amazed to see his friend lay his head on his desk. His cheek was twitching more than ever.

But by the time Bill reached the classroom door, Stan had already vanished down the hall. That afternoon, for the first time, Stan didn't show up for basketball practice.

Bill decided to telephone him that evening. He didn't often do that. It was always so hard to talk to Stan's mother. This time their conversation was briefer than usual.

"Can I talk to Stan, please?"

"He's not home."

"When do you think he'll be back?"

"I have no idea," she said sharply and hung up.

The next day, Stan suddenly appeared, his face beaming.

"How you been, Sport?"

"OK, I guess." Bill didn't really know what to say.

"Sorry I missed practice yesterday," Stan said. "Believe me, I couldn't help it." Stan seemed almost to be pleading.

Bill was feeling more and more uneasy. Then he noticed that Stan no longer wore sunglasses.

"Anything wrong with your eyes?" Bill asked. "They look watery and . . ."

But Stan quickly interrupted him. "Could you let me have a few dollars until next week?" Bill reached into his pocket. This was the second loan in the last month.

Stan took the money, flashed another big smile and walked off. "See you at practice this afternoon," he said.

"How things have changed!" thought Bill. In all the years of their friendship it was almost an unwritten agreement that they would never borrow money from each other.

But at basketball practice that afternoon, Stan seemed his old self. Only during warm-up did Bill notice that Stan's famous timing was off. He was the star of the team, but today he handled the ball hesitantly. He missed five practice shots in a row.

"Can't get them all!" Stan joked. But Bill knew he was upset.

"Anyway, I bet I can still beat you at Indian wrestling," Stan challenged. Bill accepted, secretly hoping Stan still could.

They wandered over to the coach's table. Getting into position for Indian wrestling, elbows on the table, they grasped each other's hand. At that moment, Bill felt a chill as cold, perspiring fingers clamped over his own. Stan's hand was trembling.

"Ready?" Stan asked. They began straining to pin down each other's arm. Usually the young men were well matched. Today it seemed as if all Stan's power had left him.

"Just got me off guard, Sport," Stan quickly said. "I'll beat you this time." Once more they grasped each other's hand. Stan's seemed even colder now. Bill won again without much effort.

"You're getting stronger, Sport, but you won't beat Old Powerhouse again!" For the third time, they got into wrestling position. Then suddenly Bill understood.

He had caught sight of something on Stan's arm. Hoping he had been mistaken, he looked again. But there it was. The friends' eyes met. Without a word exchanged between them, the secret was out.

Just then the coach blew the whistle to continue practice. As Stan ran off to the middle of the court, his last look seemed to say, "Forget it, Sport. There's nothing you can do."

Deeply shaken by the sight of those pinholes in Stan's arm, Bill stood in a daze as his friend grabbed a ball and tried a few more shots. None connected with the basket. The coach's yell brought Bill back to earth and onto the court.

He fumbled his way through practice, watching his friend out of the corner of his eye. Afterwards, Stan managed to duck out of the locker room without speaking to Bill.

That evening was the most troubled of Bill's life. He couldn't eat; he couldn't sit still. His mother asked him what was wrong, but he couldn't tell her, especially after what had happened to his cousin Fred.

Bill hadn't thought about Fred for a long time. Stan always reminded Bill of Fred. Both were good athletes, both had been school leaders.

Fred had a great future ahead of him, everyone had said. But that was before he had started fooling around with the *stuff*. Bill was still haunted by the memory of the night the police had come. They reported that Fred had been killed while trying to rob a gas station.

Poor Fred. How hooked he must have been to do something as desperate as that!

Bill's mother had said at the time, "Someone should have called the police while there was still time to do something. He needed help!" Now, recalling those words, Bill winced. Could he turn in his best friend?

Though his heart wasn't in it, Bill decided to go to basketball practice the next day. The big game was coming up. Bill couldn't let the team down.

Once there, Bill noticed that Stan was missing. But Stan needed help badly. Bill decided then and there to find him. He left his teammates standing on the court.

He didn't have to search too far. Stan was in the dressing room going through the lockers, frantically pocketing money, watches, rings—anything.

"No, Stan, stop!" Bill shrieked, beside himself.

Stan spun around. He was wearing sunglasses again. His hands were shaking badly and sweat was rolling down his face.

"Here," Bill reached for his wallet, "I have ten dollars. Put those things back."

Stan's voice was full of despair. "That just isn't enough."

"Remember what happened to Fred," Bill pleaded.

"Yeah, I know. But that won't happen to me!"

Stan made a move to go, but Bill was determined to stop him.

"You better let me by, Sport," Stan said in a trembling voice.

Bill stood his ground. Stan's fist connected with Bill's stomach. Bill sagged to the floor.

As he came to, jumbled phrases floated through his mind. "Sorry, Sport . . . didn't mean . . . to hit so hard . . . you don't know . . . what it's like . . ."

Bill stumbled along the halls of the school, not knowing where he was going, tears streaming down his face. He hadn't cried like that—since Fred had been killed.

"*Someone should have called the police while there was still time to do something. He needed help!*" Again his mother's words echoed through his mind.

But how could you do that to a friend?

Suddenly Bill saw a phone booth at the end of the hall. All he had to do was dial and say. "My friend is . . . is . . . a dope addict!"

The phone booth seemed to grow larger and larger. Bill stood still for a moment. Then . . .

Annotations

buddy *Am.* friend – **first grade** *Am.* first school year – **to startle** to shock – **to slump** *here:* to sit in a bent, lazy position – **tuned out** *sl.* not paying attention – **to twitch** to make a sudden, uncontrollable movement – **to amaze** [ə'meiz] to surprise greatly – **to vanish** to disappear – **brief** short – **to hang up** *here:* to end a telephone call – **to beam** *here:* to smile happily – **how you been?** *sl.* how have you been – **I guess** *sl.* I suppose – **to plead** to beg – **uneasy** [–'–] worried – **Indian wrestling** ['resliŋ] test of strength, using the hand and arm – **coach** trainer – **to grasp** to seize firmly – **chill** cold sensation – **to perspire** [pəs'paiə] to sweat – **to clamp over** to hold tightly – **to tremble**

to shake – **to grab** to take roughly – **yell** shout – **to fumble** to use the hands without skill – **to duck out** to get out quickly without being seen – **locker room** room where the players change – **the stuff** *here:* drugs – **to haunt** [hɔːnt] *here:* to keep coming back to the mind – **gas** *Am.* petrol – **hooked** *sl.* unable to stop doing s.th.; *here:* unable to stop taking drugs – **to recall** to remember – **to wince** [wins] to show signs of (*here:* mental) pain – **to turn s.o. in** to inform on s.o. (to the police etc.) – **frantically** wildly – **to shriek** to scream – **beside o.s.** no longer having any self-control – **to spin, spun (around)** to turn around quickly – **yeah** [jɛə] *sl.* yes – **you better** *sl.* you'd better – **to sag** to sink down – **jumbled** ['dʒʌmbld] mixed-up – **to stumble along** to walk in an unsteady way – **dope addict** ['ædikt] person who is unable to stop taking drugs

Questions on the story

1. Why is Bill so worried about Stan?
2. What is, in fact, wrong with Stan? When does Bill realize this?
3. In what way does Stan remind Bill of Fred? Why does Bill think of Fred now?
4. What do you think Bill's and Stan's home lives are like? What clues are there in the text?
5. What happens in the dressing room the next day?
6. How would you describe Bill's feelings at the end?

What happens now?

1. What can Bill do now? Discuss the various possibilities.
2. What would you do in Bill's position, and why?
3. Complete the story in your own words:
   'Bill stood still for a moment. Then . . .'

Run, Baby, Run

"It's not every day you get invited to a fancy restaurant, baby," Harris said to himself as he made his way along the crowded sidewalk. For him this was going to be one beautiful day. He stopped for a moment to admire the reflection of his new suit in a store window. "Not bad at all." It was the first he'd ever bought with his own money.

But why was he walking here today? It had been more than five years since he'd passed through the ghetto. But here he was, bumping against people and looking around. Same old buildings about to fall apart. Same old trash in the streets. Same old smells of stale food. Nothing had changed, and Harris almost felt he missed it. He had had some good times in the ghetto and he still felt drawn to it.

But could it ever get him back? Those filthy hallways. All those poor people crowded together in those rotting tenements. The sad old folks sitting out on their stoops just staring. Why, there wasn't even enough room in the streets to move around.

And the kids! Harris could tell which of them were already headed for trouble. He had spent enough of his life in the streets and in a reform school to know all the signs.

The sights and the memories were now beginning to get to him. He didn't want to feel low, especially today. And what if he ran into someone he knew? What would he have to say after all those years? He began walking faster. Without realizing it, he was almost running. He just had to get away from all this . . .

Before he knew it, he was passing through clean, quiet streets. There were trees planted along the curbs, and even the air smelled cleaner. The ghetto was far behind him, and soon his depressed feelings left him. He slowed down.

But he still arrived at the restaurant much too soon. Jim wouldn't be there for another half-hour at least. To pass the time, he watched the people as they entered the restaurant. He was relieved to see a few black faces among them. Harris still wasn't completely at ease in the white world. "Baby, you'd probably be more sure of yourself washing the dishes in there," he laughed to himself. As a matter of fact, he had worked as a dishwasher several times in the last few years. But he didn't regret it one bit.

"Whew, just look at those prices!" he said to himself, inspecting the menu in the window. But then Jim wouldn't celebrate this day in any other way. Nothing but the best for a good friend on a special occasion.

Jim was such a great guy. Harris wondered what his life would have been like without him. He hadn't especially liked Jim at first. Harris had thought he was just another reform school counselor who didn't know the score.

But he soon found out that Jim was different. Maybe it was because Jim had also come up the hard way and understood what Harris had gone through, and what he still had to do.

Many times Jim had told Harris, "You know, baby, it's up to you."

"Don't hand me that. There ain't no place out there for me. All they have to do is look at me. They've got their minds made up already."

"Listen, baby," Jim insisted, "give yourself a chance. Think as much of yourself as you want others to think of you."

Talks like that had pulled Harris through. Now he knew he'd done the right thing. He'd had enough of reform schools.

Two years before, when Harris had been released, Jim had taken time off to help him find a good place to live. "To make sure you get a new start," he had said, "we've got to keep you out of the ghetto." For Harris it had been strange, at first, living in a neighborhood where the faces weren't all black. He had gotten used to it, though, and he hardly ever thought about the old streets and the old ways. And when he sometimes felt he couldn't make it, Jim was always there to turn to.

They'd been hard years in other ways too. Low-paying jobs with long hours—dishwasher, busboy, porter. All so that he could get a high school diploma. But on the day he walked up to the platform to receive it, Jim had also been there. Harris couldn't have felt prouder.

And now Jim would be there to help him celebrate this biggest day of all. Had Harris ever imagined the time would come when he'd be graduating from a police academy?

He was never quite sure why he had made the decision to become a policeman. Sometimes he thought it was a way of getting back onto those streets—where the kids were. He knew the ghetto and he had paid its price. Maybe he could help keep some of those kids up there from paying it too. Maybe he could be to them what Jim had been to him.

Just then, Harris's thoughts were sharply interrupted by a shrill cry, "Help! Thief! My purse!" He turned just in time to see a black girl snatch away an elderly white woman's purse. Then the girl flew past him, pursued by the woman. Immediately, Harris took after them. The woman was rapidly running out of breath and he passed her. But the girl was something else. Man, could she run! But Harris finally caught up to her. He grabbed her arm. But she shook him off. Still, he kept after her. At last, he had her!

"Let me go! Let me go!" she screamed and sobbed at the same time. He clutched her tightly by the arms and held her against a car.

Harris looked at her. There was a desperate, dull look in her eyes. He knew that look from the past. She was on something . . .

She began to struggle. He held her tighter. "Why you doing this?" she wept. A group of people were slowly gathering around them. Harris noticed a few black faces among them. And then he realized like a shot that they must have been part of the *gang*. He knew what

they were up to. It was called "Working Main Street." And he had taken part in it many times himself.

He looked at the girl's hands. Sure enough, she didn't have the purse. After all, you don't get caught holding the evidence. Harris could have kicked himself for missing that trick. He knew it well enough. He had been sent to reform school the last time for not being fast enough on a job just like this. The girl had tossed the purse to someone in the gang while she was running. He had handed it to someone else, and so forth, until someone got it who could walk away unnoticed.

"What's going on here?" said a policeman as he edged towards them through the crowd.

"Everything under control. Patrolman Brown, here . . ." Harris was about to say. But another voice broke in.

"My purse! My purse!" Harris recognized the woman's voice. She too was pushing her way through the crowd. "Where is she . . . There she is . . . She took it . . . That *nigger* . . ."

That nigger! That was all Harris had to hear. It was as if she'd spat in his face. "That nigger, that nigger." Enraged, he kept repeating it to himself. "People like her don't deserve to be helped. Why am *I* doing it?" Suddenly, he dropped the girl's arms and let himself be swallowed up in the crowd.

But for some reason, he didn't make his escape. He stood to the side, watching, listening. There was a lot of confusion. Everybody told his own version of the story. Shortly, they'd have to let the girl go. There was no case against her without evidence and without a witness. Harris was the only witness.

But then he heard that woman's voice again, higher than all the others. "And then some colored man . . ."

"*Colored man! Me!*" To Harris that was almost worse than *nigger.*

"Calm down, lady," he heard the policeman say. "Can you identify the man who caught the girl?"

There was silence as the white woman looked from black face to black face. For a second, her eyes stopped as she looked at Harris. Then she turned to the policeman and said, "No, I just can't tell. They all look alike . . ."

For Harris that was the last straw. "Her and her stupid white mind. *They all look alike!* Why she's no better than the girl who stole her purse. Worse!" He turned away in fury.

But in that instant, Harris suddenly found himself face to face with—Jim! On the other side of the crowd. It was him all right. But how long had he been there? Had he seen the whole thing?

Of course he had. Harris could tell. And he had understood the whole thing. Now Harris looked Jim straight in the eye. Would Jim give him some hint about what to do?

But Jim's expression said only one thing. "Baby, I can't help you out on this one. It's up to you . . ."

Harris took a step toward the crowd. He was not really sure of what he was doing. He looked from the shrieking white woman to the sobbing black girl. All he had to do now was walk away . . . or turn to the policeman. Suddenly, he made up his mind. He . . .

Annotations

baby *sl. here:* man – **fancy** *here:* expensive – **sidewalk** *Am.* pavement – **trash** rubbish – **stale** not fresh – **filthy** very dirty – **to rot** to go bad – **tenement** ['–––] large building divided into flats – **stoop** *here: Am.* small raised terrace at the entrance of a house – **to stare** [stɛə] to look for a long time with wide-open eyes – **kid** *colloq.* child or young person – **to head for** to be going in the direction of – **reform school** prison for young people – **to get to** *here:* to make an impression on – **low** *here:* sad – **to run into s.o.** to meet s.o. unexpectedly – **curb** (also: **kerb**) edge of a pavement – **whew** [hwuː] sound expressing surprise – **counselor** ['kaunsələ] *here:* person who offers advice – **didn't know the score** was naive; wasn't aware of the real problem – **ain't** *sl.* isn't – **to pull through** to come safely through (a crisis etc.) – **to release** [ri'liːs] to set free – **gotten** *Am.* got – **to make it** to succeed – **busboy** *Am.* waiter's helper in a restaurant – **platform** ['––] *here:* flat structure raised above floor-level for speakers in a hall etc. – **to graduate** ['grædjueit] – **shrill** high and sharp in sound – **purse** *Am.* handbag – **to snatch** to take s.th. quickly – **to pursue** [pə'sjuː] to go after in order to catch (s.o., s.th.) – **to take after** *here:* to go after – **something else** *sl.* something special; amazing – **to grab** to seize roughly – **to sob** to draw in o.'s breath while crying – **to clutch** to take hold of – **why you doing this?** *sl.* why are you doing this? – **to weep, wept** to cry – **like a shot** suddenly – **what they were up to** what they were doing – **to toss** to throw – **to edge** to move slowly forward or along – **nigger** impolite word for a Negro or member of any dark-skinned race – **enraged** [in'reidʒd] very angry – **fury** ['fjuəri] great anger – **hint** indirect suggestion – **to shriek** to scream

Questions on the story

1. What do we learn about Harris's early life?
2. What are his feelings towards the ghetto?
3. Who is Jim? How did he help Harris?
4. Why is Harris going to meet Jim today?
5. What happens on the way?
6. What do you understand by: 'She was on something ...' (p. 13, l. 17)?
7. Why does the girl no longer have the purse?
8. Why doesn't Harris tell the policeman what happened?
9. What stops Harris from walking away?
10. How does Jim react?

What happens now?

1. What important decision must Harris make at the end? Why does he hesitate?
2. Tell in your own words what you think Harris finally decides to do: 'Suddenly he made up his mind. He ...'
3. Explain why you think he makes this decision.

But I Didn't Know

Marge was in one of her moods again. "Nothing to do . . . same old stuff." The angrier she got, the faster she pedaled. Each turning of the wheels cried out, "I'm bored! I'm bored! I *must* get away! I *must* get away!" Without realizing it, she turned her bike into Hillside Park.

There were many things Marge wanted to forget. School!—a real bore . . . useless junk . . . a bunch of teachers who couldn't care less about her. Friends!—a real joke. Empty talk . . . same faces . . . same everything. And guys!—all with one thing on their minds. And Larry wasn't any different.

The hill was getting steep. Marge struggled along, thinking about things at home. She didn't care for her father. He just sat glued to the television set and only stopped for another beer. "Shut up! Can't you see I'm busy?" was the only conversation he made with her. As for her mother, she almost didn't exist. About all she ever had to say was, "Sorry, Marge, there's too much work to be done. We'll talk later." Later never came.

"At last." Marge gave a sigh of relief. The top of the hill. A chance to be alone and forget for a while. Marge's Hilltop. No one else allowed.

She leaned the bike against the tree and climbed onto a large rock. Marge's Throne. There, she loved to look down at the houses and think that people below didn't know she was watching them.

Suddenly she had a strange feeling that she wasn't alone. At first, she was afraid. Then she became a little curious.

Slowly, cautiously, she looked around. Someone else *was* here. Worst of all, a guy! He had no right to be on her private hilltop!

But the young man didn't even seem to realize she was there. He was reading. Something called "Civilization." "Who would want to read that stuff!" she thought. "Ugh!"

Marge stretched out near the rock. The sun felt good on her face. It was the first real spring day. The hill seemed so beautiful that she nearly forgot her problems. The buds in the trees had just begun to bloom, splashing yellows and reds and purples against every possible shade of green. Marge suddenly wished she knew what kind of trees they were. Why hadn't she learned *that* in science class instead of having to label those silly carrots?

The silence was broken by music. She looked around. It couldn't be! The young man had a transistor radio. And he was listening to *that* kind of music—the stuff Mrs Able, the music teacher, said the class ought to appreciate. Marge almost laughed out loud—only squares listen to that kind of music!

Then she noticed that the young man had picked up something. It was a bird, though she hadn't been sure at first. At that moment he looked up and found her watching him. He gave a quick smile. Marge turned away. But curiosity got the better of her.

She walked over. He looked up and smiled again. Then he turned his attention to the bird. "Its leg is broken. It must have fallen from the tree," he said, gravely.

Marge watched him make a splint of twigs for the bird's leg and carefully wrap a piece of his handkerchief around it. Then he gently stroked its head and said, "You'll be all right soon." He put the bird down in the grass, and he and Marge watched as it hopped around as best it could. "It's horrible to be lame," he said.

And then suddenly remembering himself, he laughed and said, "Oh, I'm sorry. My name is Pete."

"I'm Marge." She hesitated a few moments. "Can I tell you something?"

"Sure."

"You know, I was very angry when I first saw you here. I come here a lot and I'm almost always alone. I think of it as my own private place."

Pete's face expressed worry. "Oh, I didn't mean anything personal," said Marge. "I just didn't want anyone around. But I'm glad you're here," she added quickly, "really I am."

The hill was quiet. Pete's smile returned. The bird was still hopping around. "How did you know how to fix the bird's leg?" Marge broke the silence.

"I know a little about birds. My hobby is training pigeons."

"Oh!" Marge was surprised. She had never known anyone interested in training pigeons. "What do you do with them?"

He told her about training birds: "I feel an excitement each time I see the birds take off, free for a while, flying where they want."

Marge listened closely, because of the way he explained it, because he made her feel a part of what he was saying.

"You must like nature a lot," Marge said. "I wish I knew more about nature. I was looking at the trees before and realized how little I knew about them. See how smart I am!"

Pete began to name the trees and tell her some things about them, but suddenly he stopped. "There I go again. I must be boring you."

"Oh, no, please go on, Pete," Marge said. She really meant it. She had never really seen trees the way Pete was helping her to see them today.

Marge had never thought the afternoon would turn out so enjoyable. Even the music pleased her.

"What are they playing?" she asked.

"One of my favorites. Beethoven's Ninth Symphony," he answered. "Did you know that Beethoven was completely deaf when he wrote that music? It's amazing how someone can overcome a handicap. Maybe our bird will have a chance to survive."

"Pete, you know, you're amazing. I don't think I've ever known anybody who was interested in so many things. I bet you never get bored."

Pete smiled, "Sometimes you have to get interested in things. Otherwise you have too much time to feel sorry for yourself."

"I'll bet you're not a basketball fan," Marge said, thinking how much Larry and her father were interested in sports.

"I can't *play* basketball," Pete said, lowering his eyes, "but I'm a great spectator."

There was silence between them for a few moments.

"Marge," he said, finally, "I think *you* are an amazing person. You're one of the few people I've really been able to talk to. I'm pretty much of a loner. That's why I've had to learn so many things."

Marge suddenly understood. No wonder she felt so comfortable with Pete even though she had just met him. She, too, was a loner, though she hadn't admitted it to herself before. Pete had helped her really see herself for the first time.

Marge laughed. They both laughed. It was the kind of laughing that said they shared a secret about each other. Something like this would never happen with Larry.

Then Marge realized it was late. "It's 5:30. I have to be going."

"I'm sorry. Will I be able to see you again?" asked Pete.

Marge made a quick decision. "Pete, the rec center is having a dance Saturday night. My boyfriend Larry is tied up with a basketball awards dinner. Could I ask you to go with me?"

"Gee, that would be great, but I'd be no fun at a dance."

A look of disappointment came over Marge's face. But Pete continued, "What if I got tickets for the rock concert at the stadium for Sunday night?"

"Pete, I'd love it."

"Suppose I call you at 6:30 and tell you the details."

He handed Marge a pencil and paper. While she was writing her address and telephone number, Marge saw a big man get out of a car and walk toward them with a warm smile.

"It's my father," Pete said. "He's come to pick me up." He introduced them.

And then it happened. Pete's father leaned forward and lifted Pete up from the ground. Then the big man supported him slowly to the car. Marge's eyes widened when she saw the brace on Pete's left leg dragging across the grass.

Pete leaned out of the car window to remind her about calling her at 6:30. Then the car was gone. Marge sat down, tears streaming down her cheeks.

Then she became angry with herself. Why hadn't she understood some of the things he was saying . . . the lame bird . . . the composer who overcame his handicap . . . the dance . . . basketball. Pete hadn't tried to hide anything. The brace seemed so large and ugly as he had limped away.

She realized that he had talked about himself that way because he thought she understood. How could she have been so blind? Then she realized! She had made a date with a . . . a cripple. What would the others say when they saw her with him Sunday? And what about Larry? Every eye would be on her as she and Pete entered, his left leg dragging in that brace. All of those whispers, and the noise of the brace against the floor.

Marge was so dazed that she didn't realize that she had pedaled the long way home. It was after 6:30 when she got there.

Even her mother was concerned. "Marge, where have you been? Your dinner is cold. By the way," she added, "there was a call for you about ten minutes ago. Some young man. But he said he'd call back again."

Just then the telephone rang. Marge's heart seemed to miss a beat. It rang again. Then she heard her mother say, "Marge . . . just a minute . . . Marge! Telephone for you."

Marge picked up the receiver and heard Pete say, "Hi, Marge! It's all set for Sunday. My father will pick you up at 7:30. OK?"

Marge swallowed hard—then said, "Pete . .

Annotations

to bore to make s.o. tired and unhappy by talk, work etc. which is very uninteresting – **junk** things of little or no value – **guy** [gai] *Am.* man, fellow – **steep** (of a hill) rising or falling sharply – **glued to** *here:* unable to look away from – **shut up!** *sl.* be quiet! – **ugh!** [əːh] expression of dislike – **bud** leaf, flower or branch at the beginning of its growth – **to label** [ˈleibl] to put a piece of paper etc. on s.th. to show what it is – **square** *here:* person considered to be old-fashioned – **grave** serious – **splint** piece of wood etc. bound to an arm, leg etc. to keep a broken bone in the right position – **twig** small branch of a tree or bush – **smart** *here:* clever – **deaf** [def] unable to hear – **amazing** very surprising – **to survive** [səˈvaiv] to continue to live – **spectator** [spekˈteitə] person watching a game etc. – **loner** *Am.* person who avoids the company of other people – **rec center** *colloq.* recreation center: place where informal dances, games etc. are held – **award** [əˈwɔːd] prize – **to call** *here:* to telephone – **brace** support – **to drag** *here:* to be drawn along the ground – **to limp** to walk lamely – **dazed** unable to think clearly – **receiver** *here:* part of the telephone that is held to the ear

Questions on the story

1. Why does Marge often go to Hillside Park?
2. Who does she find on her 'private hilltop' today? What is her first reaction?
3. What brings them together? How does Marge's attitude change?
4. Why does she find the afternoon so enjoyable?
5. In what ways do they find each other 'amazing'? What do they have in common?
6. What does Marge suggest they do on Saturday?
7. What is Pete's reaction? What does he suggest they do instead?
8. What makes Marge cry?
9. What are Marge's first thoughts when she realizes what she has agreed to?
10. Why is it after 6:30 when Marge arrives home?

What happens now?

1. Which of the following alternatives do you think Marge will take, and why?
   a) She agrees to go out with Pete.
   b) She decides not to go and makes up an excuse.
   c) She decides not to go and tells him the real reason.
   How do you think Pete would react to b) or c)?
2. Now complete the telephone conversation between Marge und Pete: 'Marge swallowed hard – then said, "Pete . . .'

Not Like Jeff

Stevie's angry again. After school he usually comes into the kitchen for milk and cookies. Today he just storms into the house and runs upstairs without even saying hello. What a moody boy! Who knows what's bothering him this time! I'll just ignore him. He'll cool off. Then maybe he'll come downstairs and tell me what it's all about.

It's funny how different Jeff is from Stevie. I'm their mother, but sometimes I find it hard to believe they're brothers. Jeff seems so much older, though they're only two years apart.

But then Jeff always makes a better impression. "A real movie star," Aunt Lil calls him. "Our own little football pro," Uncle Benjie says. A fine boy. Friendly. Outgoing. The whole family agrees.

Now Stevie—when there's company, he's up in his room drawing. And if he comes downstairs, he just looks at magazines while everybody is talking. Aunt Lil asks him how he's doing in school and he shrugs and says, "OK." Uncle Benjie asks him if he saw the Lion-Colt game and of course he says no. Stevie's not interested in sports. He doesn't even like to watch TV. He doesn't like anything other kids like.

It's Jeff who does the talking. Baseball. Football. Basketball. He knows every team, every score, all the averages. He plays on two varsity teams himself and he could be on others, but he just doesn't have enough time.

After all, he's class president and president of the school debating club. And if that weren't enough, he's pulling an A average and still manages to earn extra spending money. His father and I allow him to work part-time at the drugstore. We'd prefer he didn't, but he's such a capable boy . . .

Stevie struggles along in school. Not even a B average. His teachers can't understand why. During her last conference with us, Stevie's science teacher, Mrs Jones, asked him why he didn't work as hard as his brother Jeff. Do you know, that boy just picked himself up in the middle of what she was saying and walked out of the room. I made him apologize to her the next day.

But that's the sort of thing he does. Funny things bother him. He sticks to himself, and he draws. That seems to be the only thing he really seems to care about. It's the only subject in school where he gets A's.

His art teacher even sent us a note telling us we ought to encourage him. Oh, we try. But how can you get excited over a drawing of a bowl of apples? Jeff always tells Stevie that he likes his pictures. Jeff is such a kind boy.

Well, other people like Stevie's drawings too. One of his pictures is in a display of school art at the department store. It isn't a bad picture at all. We all went to see it the first day it was hanging—the same day we celebrated Jeff's big debating club victory. What a debate that was! I've never been so proud of him!

But it's that department store that's also caused all this bother. It's giving a dinner honoring those students whose work is on display. We were even sent special invitations. But wouldn't you know, Jeff's playing in *the* big game in Carsonville tonight. I told Stevie last night that we can't go to both. My husband feels one of us should go to the game and the other to the dinner. Of course, we'd rather go to the game. I wonder if Stevie would be all that hurt if we didn't go to that dinner.

Oh my! He's coming downstairs now. What should I tell him?

Annotations

cookie ['kuki] *Am.* small, flat cake – **moody** temperamental; bad-tempered – **to bother s.o.** ['bɔðə] to worry s.o. – **to cool off** to become calm – **movie** ['mu:vi] *Am.* film – **pro** *colloq.* professional – **outgoing** ['–ˌ–] friendly, interested in other people – **to shrug** to lift o.'s shoulders – **varsity** *Am.* first team representing a college or university in a sport – **pulling an A average** getting good marks in all subjects – **drugstore** *Am.* shop which sells medicine etc. and usually serves light meals – **capable** ['keipəbl] able – **to apologize** [ə'pɔlədʒaiz] to say sorry – **department store** large shop which sells many different kinds of goods – **bother** trouble – **oh my!** dear me!

Questions on the story

1. In what ways is Stevie different from Jeff?
2. What is the one thing that Stevie is really interested in?
3. Why do his parents find it difficult to encourage him?
4. How does Jeff react to Stevie's pictures?
5. What is the problem that has to be solved?

What happens now?

1. Do you agree with the father's suggestion that one parent should go to the game and one to the dinner? Why?/Why not?
   If not, what do you think they should do, and why?
2. Imagine that Stevie has come downstairs in a very bad temper. Write the dialogue that might be spoken by Stevie and his mother.
3. Jeff has been listening to this dialogue. What does he say to his mother/to Stevie?

Wendy

If you don't want to hear my side of this story, you can just close your book—if your teacher will let you. But then you'll never know why I feel Wendy's wrong—and why Wendy feels she's right.

Wendy's in high school, and she's really just like any other kid her age. At least that's what I think, and I ought to know. I'm her father. Well, you be the judge.

Wendy's got a sister named Karen. She goes to a college that's just fifteen minutes from home. But I spend $500 extra every year so that she can live in a dorm. You see, we want her to have a good social life . . .

But I'm only telling you this to show how much we care about our kids. Wendy doesn't have anything to complain about, either. We live in a beautiful house in the suburbs and she gets more spending money than most girls her age do.

Still, Wendy has always been a problem. Ever since she started school, her teachers have been telling us how bright she is. That's just great. But then we'd get notes from them that began: "I would like to have a conference with you."

Then we'd hear that Wendy wasn't doing quite as well as we thought. "It's really not her work," they'd say. "It's her attitude . . ." Maybe Wendy is too bright for her own good.

So I asked Wendy. "What's the problem?"

"Oh, it's those dumb teachers," she'd answer. "They just don't know what they're teaching."

Now you figure that out. These people go to college for four years, and then this kid says they don't know anything! But that's not all she had to say.

"And they always ask us to do dumb things. They make us read textbooks that don't mean anything to us. And when we ask them, 'Why can't we talk about *important* things for a change?' they just tell us we don't know what's important. Or they say we have to stick to our program of study."

She likes only one teacher. Her social studies teacher. But I know that man. He's a real weirdo. They should fire him. Wendy probably gets all her crazy ideas from him.

But that's beside the point. Wendy isn't really old enough to decide what she should be learning in school. When I was her age, I never questioned what the teachers did or said. I went to school to learn. But most kids today go to school to fool around. It's like a social club for them.

If it was up to her, Wendy would just "rap" all day about politics or ecology—all kinds of things she doesn't really know anything about. Thank goodness there are a few students left who aren't that way.

Excuse me a minute. I'll be back. Wendy just came in . . .

Well, this is the last straw! Wendy just got home from school with a note for me to sign. I have to give her permission to . . . You won't believe this. Her nutty social studies teacher is working on some project called "Modern Problems" or something like that. And he wants these school kids to organize—a protest march!

Right! A protest march! They're supposed to demonstrate in front of some factory downtown that's been polluting the air. Then they've made arrangements to speak to two state senators. These kids! Did you ever hear anything like it? They think they're going to change the world overnight. High school kids should have other things on their minds and leave the protesting to us adults.

But what really shocks me is that the school is actually encouraging them. It ought to know better. A school's business is to teach

American history and science and math, not to get its students involved in foolishness.

Wendy will probably be out there in front. I find it harder and harder to reason with that girl.

Well, do you see now what's wrong with Wendy? I have a feeling that most of you are not like her. How about taking some time to discuss her problem?

Annotations

kid *colloq.* child or young person – **dorm** *colloq.* dormitory; *here:* building at a college where students live – **suburb** [ˈsʌbəːb] district just outside a city or town – **bright** *here:* clever – **attitude** way of thinking or behaving – **dumb** *here: sl.* stupid – **weirdo** [ˈwiədəu] strange or eccentric person – **crazy** *sl.* mad – **beside the point** not relevant – **to rap** *sl.* to talk – **ecology** [iˈkɔlədʒi] science which deals with the relation between living things and their surroundings – **the last straw** s.th. which makes an already bad situation unbearable – **nutty** *sl.* mad – **to pollute** [pəˈluːt] to make dirty

Questions on the story

1. Why does Karen live in a dorm, although her college is only fifteen minutes from home?
2. What sort of social background do you think the family comes from?
3. Why is Wendy a problem, according to her father?
4. Which teacher does Wendy like?
5. What is Wendy interested in?
6. What are the school kids supposed to organize, and why? Whose idea is it?
7. What sort of person is Wendy/Wendy's father? Support your answers with quotes from the text.

What happens now?

1. When you have discussed this problem, write a letter to Wendy's father, telling him what you think of Wendy and of his attitude. Begin: 'Dear Mr Gilmore,'
2. Mr Gilmore must also decide whether or not to give Wendy permission to take part in the project. Write a possible dialogue between Wendy and her father on this subject.

The Man with the Cigar

Paul sat in the waiting room. He was feeling more and more impatient. Every time someone in white passed by, he jumped up from his chair. Dr Jones had said that the operation would only take an hour, but three hours had already passed and still there was no news.

Paul knew he'd better stop walking back and forth to the water fountain when he wasn't even thirsty. He had to relax. In the condition he was in, he would never be any help to his team in the big game.

Still no sign of Dr Jones. Paul sat back and looked around the waiting room. Most of the people who had been there earlier had already gone. The only ones left were a boy and his father—and the man with the cigar.

Who was he? When Paul had arrived at the hospital early that morning, the man was already there, sitting in the same chair. He seemed to move only to flick the ashes off the end of his cigar. Paul didn't know why, but he was beginning to feel annoyed by that man and his cigar.

Paul picked up a magazine, but he couldn't concentrate. Suddenly, he heard a voice. "You're Paul Johnson, aren't you?" Paul looked up. The boy had come over and was standing before him.

"Yeah, I am." Paul smiled—he always enjoyed being recognized. "How do you know my name?"

"Oh, I've seen your picture on the sports page lots of times," the boy answered, "and I watch you play in all the games. My father is taking me this afternoon to see you in the state championship."

"That's great!" Paul liked the boy. "I'll make my first touchdown today just for you."

The boy's face lit up. "Gee!" he said. "Someday I'm going to be on the football team. I want to be as great a star as you are—or like my dad was—Matt Holmes . . ."

"Wow!" said Paul excitedly. "Is your father Matt Holmes?" Everyone had heard of Matt. He was almost a legend. He had been Central High's most famous athlete.

"Yes," said the boy proudly. "And I'm Matt Junior. But everybody calls me 'Chip' because I'm supposed to be a chip off the old block!" Matt smiled from across the room and got up to join them.

Paul enjoyed talking with the great Matt Holmes. The time flew by, and Paul began to feel much less tense. Before long they were talking like old friends. Matt told Paul about his wife's operation. Paul told Matt about his hopes of going to State University the next fall and of someday playing pro football.

Then Paul began to admit how worried he felt about his mother. "I just can't understand why she's been in that operating room so long."

Suddenly, a man in white entered the waiting room. "That's my wife's doctor," Matt said.

Good news! Matt's wife was doing fine. Matt and the boy could go up and see her.

"Well, good-by son," said Matt. "Hope everything goes well with your mother. Hope we'll be seeing you at the game this afternoon, too."

"And don't forget that touchdown you promised me," Chip added.

"I won't," Paul replied, trying to smile. He watched them disappear down the hall. Now he felt alone again. But that man with the cigar was still sitting there. There was a long silence. Suddenly the man smiled at Paul, showing yellow, stained teeth. Paul felt very uncomfortable.

At that very moment, Dr Jones entered. His expression was grave. Paul could tell that the news wasn't going to be good. "She's doing fine now," the doctor said. "But there were a few problems that we couldn't foresee until we operated."

"Will she be all right?"

"I think so. She'll have to take it easy, though. It'll be some time before she can go back to work. And . . . we're going to have to get a practical nurse to stay with her for a while. It's all going to run into a lot of money, I'm afraid. Is there anyone in your family who can help?"

"No, sir, there isn't." Paul lowered his eyes. "There isn't anyone left on my mother's side, and we haven't seen much of my father's family since he died . . . But the football season will soon be over; then I can get a job right away. I'll just have to put off college for a year . . ." Paul couldn't speak any more. He was afraid his voice would give away his feelings.

"I'm sorry, son," Dr Jones said understandingly as he shook Paul's hand.

"Can I see Mom now?" asked Paul.

"No, she's still in the recovery room," said Dr Jones. "I doubt if she'll be out before late evening."

Sad and disappointed, Paul left the waiting room. Soon he was outside on the street, not quite knowing where he was going or why. Suddenly he looked at his watch. Only two hours before the game, and he hadn't eaten a thing all day. At that moment, Paul smelled something familiar. Sure enough, the man with the cigar was standing a few yards away from him. "Is he following me?" Paul asked himself in amazement.

The man took the cigar out of his mouth. "Hello, Paul," he said. "Sorry to hear about your mother. I wonder if we could have a little talk. Can I buy you some lunch?"

The man was short and fat. He wore glasses so thick that Paul could hardly see his eyes. There was something a little scary about him. "Sorry, I'm in a big hurry," said Paul. "Got to run now." He dashed quickly across the street as the light changed. Then he turned the corner and entered the nearest lunchroom.

Soon after he was seated at the counter, Paul smelled that odor once again. He looked around and found the man with the cigar seated on the stool beside him. "I'll take a cup of black coffee," said the man to the waitress.

"What do you want?" Paul finally asked angrily.

"Calm down, kid. I'm here to help you. I'm a great football fan, you know. And I've been watching your career pretty closely . . ."

There was a pause. The man drew closer to Paul and began to speak in a low voice. "You know, I heard what the doctor told you. What a shame to have to give up your football career, and the way things are going, you may never get to the university."

"What's it to you?" growled Paul.

"Money, right? You need it; I've got it."

Paul was getting angrier by the minute. "You're not offering something for nothing. What's in it for you?"

"Well, son . . ." The waitress brought them their orders, then left. "Well, son . . . there's a little something you could do. It pays well.

And if you do it right, there might be even more money . . . especially when you get to State . . ."

"And what exactly do I have to do for you, Mister?"

"Simple," the man replied. "You miss a couple of passes this afternoon. You get paid. Understand?"

Paul couldn't believe his ears. "You're kidding . . ."

"Listen, kid. A cool thousand will buy a lot of medical help."

"A thou . . ." Paul had heard that people were always trying to fix ball games, but no one had ever approached him before. He was frightened, but he was also angry. "You know, people like you should be arrested," he said. He took a dollar out of his wallet, slapped it on the counter and left without finishing his lunch.

Paul was upset. He decided to walk all the way to the stadium in hopes that it would help him calm down. When he got to the locker room, most of his teammates were already in uniform. They were sorry to hear about his mother.

Paul got into his uniform and warmed up as much as he could. He did a little running and caught a few passes. But something seemed

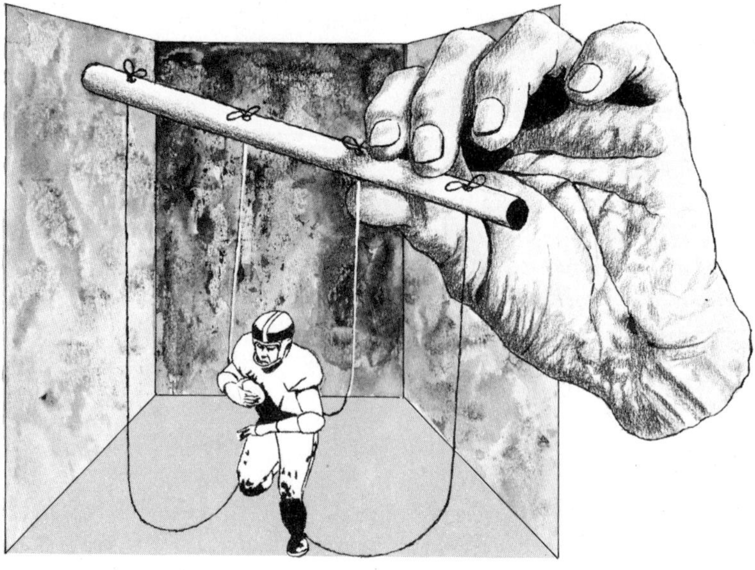

to be wrong. His timing was off. His muscles just weren't obeying him. He was too tense. His mother . . . that man with the cigar . . . He just had to get all that out of his mind!

The signal came and the team ran out on the field. The crowd cheered. Paul usually loved the cheers, but today he had a feeling that they might not be cheering at the end of the game.

The roar died down. Suddenly Paul heard someone yell, "Yeah, Paul!" Then he saw Chip in the stands, waving wildly. Matt was at his side. Paul felt a little better. He smiled and waved back at them.

Then Paul caught sight of someone else. He was sitting just a couple of rows behind Chip and Matt. Paul could almost smell the smoke of that cigar in his mouth.

The game started. Before long, Paul had the ball and was running. His confidence had returned. Then it happened. The ball just fell out of his hand. The other team got hold of it and scored their first touchdown. They kicked for the extra point and made it. That was only the first of several errors Paul made. At half time, Paul's team was losing, 14—6.

It was quiet in the locker room. For the first time that season, Central was not leading at half time. Nobody blamed Paul, but he had let his teammates down. Paul sat in a corner by himself. Suddenly he looked up and saw Chip and Matt enter the room. "Don't worry about it, son," Matt said. "I've played worse games than that in my time. And considering how you must feel . . ."

Paul was glad they'd come. He began to relax again. When they left, he called after Chip, "Remember, that first touchdown's for you!"

But on the way to the field, Paul noticed the man with the cigar waving at him. Paul gave him a look that said, "I'm going to win this game in spite of you. You won't upset me any more."

The third quarter was like old times. Paul ran forty yards to score a touchdown. The crowd went wild, and Paul could see Chip jumping up and down, yelling at the top of his voice. Paul waved to him as if to say, "There's your touchdown, Chip."

The extra point was good. At the end of the third quarter, the score was 14—13. Central was clicking. The fourth quarter would tell.

But the fourth quarter was a tough one. With only seconds left in the game, neither side had scored. Paul's team had the ball. Their only hope was to try a long pass. Paul was wide open to receive. Then, out of the corner of his eye, Paul caught sight of the man with the cigar . . . The throw was a good one, but Paul missed. Time ran out. Central lost, 14—13.

Central had lost the game and the state championship as well. Paul felt that he just couldn't face his teammates yet. So he walked out of the stadium and to the park nearby. He took off his jersey and his shoulder pads and he threw himself on the ground. "Why? Why? Why?" he kept asking himself. "Had that man with the cigar really made me lose the game?"

He stayed there a long time. Finally, he thought he'd better get back to the locker room.

When he got there, everyone else was gone. He took off his uniform but decided not to shower. He wanted to get to the hospital as quickly as he could. Paul opened his locker to get his clothes. An envelope fell out of the locker and onto the floor and its contents spilled out. There lay ten one-hundred dollar bills!

Paul just stared at the money. Then he understood. The man with the cigar had thought that Paul had lost the game on purpose.

Paul's first thought was to go to the police and tell them everything. But would they believe him? And what about the scandal that might follow? Wouldn't people always be suspicious of him after that? And what would it all do to his mother?

But then, for a brief moment, another thought crossed his mind. If he kept the money, all his problems would be solved. No more worries about his mother's medical expenses. No more worries about going to State in the fall. After all, the game was over, and . . . Paul quickly picked up the money and stuffed it in its envelope. He hurried into his clothes. He had to get out. The envelope still in his hand, he approached the locker room exit. There, standing in the doorway, was—the man with the cigar! And for a short man, he looked very large to Paul.

With a steady, determined walk, Paul . . .

Annotations

water fountain machine containing drinking water – **to relax** *here:* to become less nervous – **to flick** to hit quickly and lightly – **to annoy**

[ə'nɔi] to do s.th. which makes another person angry – **yeah** [jεə] *sl.* yes – **touchdown** (in American football) score – **gee!** [dʒiː] **wow!** [wau] expressions of surprise, pleasure etc. – **chip** small piece – **a chip off the old block** son who is very like his father – **to fly by** *here:* to go quickly – **tense** (*here:* of nerves) tightly stretched – **fall** *Am.* autumn – **pro** *sl.* professional – **grave** serious – **to foresee** [–'–] to see in advance – **to take it easy** not to work too hard – **to run into** *here:* to amount to – **right away** immediately – **mom** *colloq.* mother – **amazement** [–'– –] great surprise – **scary** ['skεəri] *colloq.* frightening – **lunchroom** *Am.* restaurant where light meals are served – **odor** ['əudə] smell – **kid** *colloq.* child or young person – **what's it to you?** what business is it of yours? – **to growl** [graul] to make a low, angry sound – **what's in it for you?** what advantage will you gain? – **to miss a pass** to drop the ball when it is thrown to you – **to kid** to joke – **cool** *here:* putting stress on the figure, i.e. no less than $1000 – **to fix** *here:* to arrange the result in advance – **to slap** to hit with the flat of the hand; *here:* to put s.th. down with a slapping sound – **upset** [–'–] disturbed – **locker room** *here:* room where the players change into their 'uniforms' – **timing** *here:* control – **to die down** to fade – **to yell** to shout – **stands** covered sitting area in a sports stadium – **error** ['erə] mistake – **to let s.o. down** to fail to help s.o. – **to click** *here:* to play well together – **wide open to receive** in a good position to take the ball and run – **jersey** ['dʒəːzi] *here:* sports shirt – **shoulder pad** s.th. worn under the jersey to protect the shoulder – **to spill out** to fall out – **to stare** [stεə] to look for a long time with wide-open eyes – **suspicious** [səs'piʃəs] having the feeling that s.o. has done s.th. wrong – **exit** ['eksit] way out

Questions on the story

1. Why is Paul so nervous?
2. Who else is in the waiting room?
3. Why does the boy recognize Paul?
4. What is Paul doing in the afternoon? What does he promise the boy?
5. Who is the boy's father?
6. Who is left in the waiting room when the boy and his father leave?
7. What does the doctor tell Paul about his mother's condition?
8. Why would Paul have to put off college for a year?
9. What happens when Paul leaves the waiting room?
10. What does the man want Paul to do? What does he offer him in return?
11. What is Paul's reaction to the man's proposal?

12. What happens during the game? What is the final result?
13. What does Paul find in his locker after the game? Who put it there, and why?
14. What are Paul's thoughts then?
15. Who appears again at the end?

What happens now?

1. Paul has several choices:
   a) He keeps the money so that he can pay his mother's hospital bill and later go on to college.
   b) He keeps the money and agrees to meet the man again.
   c) He gives the money back to the man and says he never wants to see him again.
   d) He has a fight with the man and calls the police.

   Discuss each of the above possibilities, saying why you think he would or would not act in that way.
2. What other possibilities are there? Who might he go to for help, apart from the police?
3. Now complete the story in your own words:
   'With a steady, determined walk, Paul . . .'

Walk Proud, Be Proud

The theatre was coming into view. Pat's footsteps began to quicken. Her heart was beating fast. Her first ballet performance! She still couldn't believe it was really happening.

There was still an hour before curtain-time, but she had to get there early to take it all in. Suddenly before her was a large theatre poster. "TODAY—AMERICAN BALLET COMPANY IN SWAN LAKE," it announced. It also showed a beautiful photograph of the dancers in their costumes. Pat could hardly tear herself away. "Someday I'll be on a poster like that," she whispered to herself.

Finally, she walked through the big doors into the lobby of the theatre. She felt as if she were in an enchanted palace. Her feet sank into the deep red carpet. Huge glass lamps hung overhead. And the wide marble staircase seemed to invite her up to share a new world of dreams.

For a moment, Pat felt out of place. There were so many strange faces around her—and most of them were white. They all seemed to be staring at her and wondering. "What is that black girl doing here?" But Pat told herself it was only her imagination. So she quickly joined the line to the ticket window.

As Pat looked around she saw many other young girls. Most of them seemed so happy as they talked with one another. And how well-dressed they all were!

Pat's clothes were clean and presentable. Her mother had made sure of that. But there was no denying that they looked old-fashioned and worn. After all, they were hand-me-downs from the white families Pat's mother worked for in the suburbs. "It's not important what's on you," Pat could still hear her mother saying as she waved good-by to her that morning. "What really counts is what you've got inside. Walk proud, be proud."

In the midst of her thoughts, Pat found herself listening to a voice behind her. "And Mother," said the voice, "could we go shopping later this afternoon? I'll need a new dress for the dance . . ."

"It's just another one of those rich girls from the suburbs," Pat said to herself. But a part of her was praying that no one could see the neat mending job on the hem of her skirt.

". . . And I think I'd better have my ballet lesson changed from Wednesday to Thursday . . ." the girl continued.

Ballet lesson! Pat would have given anything to take a ballet lesson.

"And I won't be home for dinner on Friday, Mother. I had to change my date for tutoring in the city . . ."

"Oh," thought Pat, "one of *those!*" She didn't really know why, but she had always hated "those rich do-gooders." They thought they would change the world by helping some black kids a couple of days a week. Pat just couldn't help turning around to catch a glimpse of her.

The girl was blonde and very pretty. She didn't look like she had a care in the world. Pat decided she hated her, though she wasn't sure just why. Maybe it was because she seemed to have everything Pat ever wanted. Maybe it was because she was white, and seemed so smug . . .

But Pat must have looked at her strangely, or far too long, because the girl suddenly spoke to her. "Hello. My name is Linda Jackson. And this is my mother . . ."

"They must be the kind of people my mother works for," thought Pat. She felt so uncomfortable that she wished she could disappear into the ground.

"Where do you go to school?" Linda asked.

"Dunbar."

"Oh, I thought I recognized you. I tutor there on Mondays. Maybe we can get together some afternoon . . ."

"Phony! Phony!" Pat said to herself. "She talks to me for about three seconds and already she wants to be my friend! And all because I'm *black,* and people are supposed to be nice to black people these days."

"And I also take ballet lessons here in town. Maybe you'd like to come with me one day . . ." Pat thought she saw Linda's mother give her daughter a nudge that was meant to say, "*Take it easy!*"

"Go with her to her ballet lessons!" thought Pat. "Doesn't she know that poor people like me can't do things like that? Shall I tell her how many lunches I did without to save enough money to buy this ticket?"

Pat was glad she was getting close to the ticket window. Soon she'd be able to get away from that chattering Linda and her mother.

"Can I help you?" asked the man behind the window.

In a low voice she answered, "One $2.50 ticket for this afternoon's performance, please."

"Sorry. All we have left are $5.00 and $7.50 tickets."

For a moment, Pat just stood there. "Thank you," she said finally in a voice that was about to break. She was sure she was going to cry, so she moved away from the window as quickly as she could.

Just then she heard the man call out to her, "Wait a minute! I do happen to have a $2.50 ticket left . . ."

Pat's face lit up into a smile. She reached into her purse and counted out the money. It was all in nickels, dimes, and quarters. When the man handed her the ticket, she felt more pleased than she could say. She'd miss a hundred more lunches to have this feeling again!

But as she walked away, she looked at the ticket. Something was wrong! The ticket said $5.00!

When she returned to the ticket window, Linda and her mother were still there. For an instant, it crossed her mind that she ought to have said good-by to them. But she had been so confused, so happy and yet so unhappy . . .

"Pardon me, sir," she said to the ticket man, "I think you made a mistake. You gave me . . ."

"It's no mistake," he said. And then Pat noticed that he and Linda's mother exchanged a glance. All of a sudden, she realized what had happened. Pat had paid $2.50 for a $5.00 ticket because Linda's mother had somehow motioned to the man that she would pay the extra $2.50.

Pat's heart sank. But she knew what she had to do. "Walk proud, be proud," her mother had told her. "Please return my money," she said to the ticket man with all the courage she had. Then she turned and looked straight into the woman's eyes. "I may be black, but I don't have to accept charity . . ."

With trembling hands she gathered up the money and headed towards the door. She hoped she would be outside before she burst into tears. But she wasn't going to run. She was going to walk out *proud!*

Outside, on the theatre steps, she could feel the sobs shaking her whole body. Tears streamed down her cheeks. Pat sat down and let go.

Just then, she felt someone touch her shoulder. She spun around. There, standing above her, was Linda's mother. There was silence for a moment. Then their eyes met. "I'm truly sorry," the woman said in a sad voice. "I know I didn't handle that very well . . ."

Pat wiped her tears quickly and stood up. She thought for a moment, and then . . .

Annotations

ballet ['bælei] – **to tear o.s. away** [tɛə] to force o.s. to go – **lobby** *here: Am.* foyer – **enchanted** [in'tʃɑːntid] having a magic spell on it – **huge** [hjuːdʒ] very large – **marble** kind of hard stone that can be polished – **to stare** [stɛə] to look for a long time – **presentable** [pri'zentəbl] suitable to be seen – **to deny** [di'nai] to say that s.th. is not true – **hand-me-downs** ['– – –] second-hand clothes – **suburb** ['sʌbəːb] district just outside a city or town – **midst** middle – **neat** *here:* done carefully – **hem** border or edge of cloth, esp. on an article of clothing – **do-gooder**

['–'– –] *colloq.* person who does good, usually for effect – **kid** *colloq.* child or young person – **glimpse** [glimps] quick look – **smug** self-satisfied – **phony** ['fəuni] *sl.* false or insincere person – **nudge** touch given with the elbow in order to attract s.o.'s attention – **take it easy** *here:* don't go too far – **to do without s.th.** to manage without s.th. – **nickel** American coin worth 5 cents – **dime** 10 cents – **quarter** 25 cents – **instant** ['– –] moment – **glance** quick look – **charity** ['tʃæriti] *here:* act of giving money or other help to the poor – **to tremble** to shake – **to head towards** to go in the direction of – **sob** sound of breath being drawn in when s.o. is crying – **to spin, spun (around)** to turn around very quickly

Questions on the story

1. Where is Pat going? Why is she so excited?
2. Why does Pat feel out of place?
3. What did her mother tell her before she left?
4. What does Pat think of the girl who is standing behind her in the queue? Why?
5. What does the man behind the ticket window tell Pat? What is her reaction?
6. Why does he then give Pat a $5 ticket for $2.50?
7. What does Pat do when she realizes what has happened? Why?
8. What does Linda's mother do then?

What happens now?

1. Can (or should) Pat forget her pride and accept the ticket? Explain your answer. What do you think are her feelings right at the end?
2. Bearing in mind your answer to the above, complete the story in your own words:
   'Pat wiped her tears quickly and stood up. She thought for a moment, and then . . .'

Play the Game

I suppose I ought to be grateful to my Aunt Alma. She always gives my folks and me expensive gifts, like the car she promised me for my next birthday. She also pays for my summer camp, and Dad says she wants to send me to college when I graduate. But I'm beginning to think that we're something like her favorite charity. The worst of it is that she seems to think she can run our lives just because she has a lot of money.

Every year her visits get harder and harder to take. Or maybe I'm getting older and can understand things better. Like this year I could tell in advance she would be more trouble than ever. First of all, I'd never seen Mom so uptight about getting the house tidy for her. It's true that Aunt Alma has a habit of looking into drawers and even under rugs. But this time the house was already cleaner than usual.

And then one morning, Mom looked me over with a strange smile and said," Bruce, don't you think you could cut your hair this week? And maybe dress a little—differently for a change? You know how your Aunt Alma is."

That was all she said. My folks never insist on things like that. But I was a little hurt and a little mad anyway. They'd never complained about the way I look before.

As far as I was concerned, there was no decision to make. I like my hair the way it is. I brush it every morning and I wash it twice a week. You can't say it's messy just because it's long. And I take a lot of time and trouble choosing my clothes. They're in the latest style, they're comfortable, and I keep them clean. My friends think I'm a great dresser. So why should I have to cut my hair and change my clothes for Aunt Alma just because she's rich?

When Aunt Alma arrived, we really rolled out the old red carpet. And naturally she brought us a batch of expensive gifts, including an album of all nine of Beethoven's symphonies for my "cultural enrichment"—whatever that means.

Mom was right, of course. As soon as Aunt Alma saw me she almost screamed, "Look at that boy! Next thing you know he'll be taking drugs. How can people let their children go around like that?"

The next evening I found five or six boxes of new clothing on my bed. White shirts, dark, baggy pants, lots of ties—things that kids used to wear maybe twenty years ago. None of us could figure out where she got them. She had removed all the labels and tickets so that we wouldn't be able to return them. But that's OK. I won't wear them anyway.

The next thing to tick me off was what she did to my room. Aunt Alma always stays in my room because it's the biggest and sunniest in the house. One day I looked in and found she'd taken all my stuff down—my wild posters, my gadgets, even my great black light—and thrown it all out! Mom hadn't done a thing to stop her. She said that Aunt Alma thought she was doing it for my own good because "those kinds of things will just lead to drugs!"

I tried extra hard not to explode, but it was bound to happen. Of course Aunt Alma's a snob. She claims her ancestors came over on the *Mayflower*, and everyone knows that she thinks my father married beneath himself. But that's all in the family.

On Saturday my club held its meeting at my house. We're big on ecology, and right now we're working on a recycling project. "Bill who?" or "Frank who?" she asked automatically as I introduced my friends to her. And when she found out, she said, "Oh, you're Italian," or "You must be Irish."

If that wasn't bad enough, when I introduced Marv *Goldberg* to her, she said, "You're *Jewish*!" And boy, the *way* she said it! I know Marv. He was pretty upset, but he didn't show it.

I waited till that evening, when I had cooled down a little. Then I let her have it. I had thought the whole thing out. First I told her I respected her because she was an older person and my aunt, but that I had rights too. I told her my hair and my clothes and my room were personal matters that she ought to respect as much as my own parents did. Finally, I told her she had no reason to pass judgment on my friends because of their race or religion.

You would have thought she had been struck by lightning. She tore out of the place without even bothering to pack her clothes. The last thing she said to me was, "And you can forget about getting that car!"

While she was waiting for a cab my parents tried to patch things

up. They told her that young people always have had their own styles and that boys today are more mature and independent than they were a generation or two ago. But she wouldn't hear them out.

Later on, when she had gone, Dad took me aside and said he thought I should have played along with her. "Look what it can get you," he said, "if you'll just play the game."

So I'm sitting up here in my room trying to think of something to write to Aunt Alma. Mom says it has to be done. Dad leaves things up to me, but I think he more or less expects me to write. Still, I honestly don't understand what they expect me to say. They think it's important for my future that I stay on her good side. Maybe so, maybe not. And they also think it was wrong of her to say and do the things she did . . . but . . .

Well, here goes—

Dear Aunt Alma,

I'm . . .

Annotations

grateful thankful – **folks** [fəuks] *colloq.* members of o.'s family – **to graduate** ['grædjueit] *here: Am.* to pass the school-leaving examination

– **charity** ['tʃæriti] *here:* organization to which one sends money in order to help people in need – **to take** *here:* to bear – **mom** *colloq.* mother – **uptight** [ˌ–ˈ–] *sl.* very nervous – **tidy** ['taidi] in good order – **rug** small carpet – **mad** *here:* angry – **messy** dirty – **to roll out the red carpet** to welcome a visitor like a very important person – **batch** number of things – **baggy** larger than necessary and rather shapeless – **pants** *Am.* trousers – **kid** *colloq.* child or young person – **label** ['leibl] *here:* piece of paper or material with the maker's or shop's name on it – **ticket** *here:* piece of paper with the size, price etc. – **to tick s.o. off** *here: sl.* to make s.o. angry – **gadget** ['gædʒit] small piece of machinery – **it was bound to happen** it had to happen – **ancestor** ['ænsistə] person from whom one is descended – **to marry beneath o.s.** to marry s.o. of a lower social status than o.s. – **big on** *sl.* very much concerned with – **ecology** [iˈkɔlədʒi] science which deals with the relation between living things and their surroundings – **to recycle** [riːˈsaikl] to put s.th. through a process so that it can be used again – **to let s.o. have it** *here:* to tell s.o. what you think of him – **lightning** flash of bright light made by natural electricity in the sky – **to bother** ['bɔðə] to take the trouble – **cab** *Am.* taxi – **to patch things up** to repair the damage – **mature** [məˈtjuə] grown-up, sensible – **to play along with s.o.** to pretend to agree with s.o. – **to be on s.o.'s good side** to have s.o.'s approval

Questions on the story

1. Why does Bruce feel he should be grateful to his Aunt Alma?
2. What does Bruce's mother ask him to do before Aunt Alma comes?
3. How does Aunt Alma react when she sees Bruce?
4. What does Bruce find on his bed the next evening?
5. What had Aunt Alma done to Bruce's room?
6. How does she treat his friends?
7. What does Bruce say to her on Saturday evening?
8. What is Aunt Alma's reaction?
9. What does Bruce's father say to him?
10. What sort of person is Aunt Alma/Bruce? Support your answers with quotes from the text.

What happens now?

1. Do you think Bruce will 'play the game'? Why?/Why not?
2. Complete Bruce's letter to Aunt Alma:
   'Dear Aunt Alma,
   I'm . . .'

My Sister, the $3.00 Bill

I guess a brother ought to stick up for his sister, even if she is a phony like my sister Peggy. Well, maybe "phony" is a little strong, but Peggy sure can act like a $3.00 bill at times. I should know. I'm Arnie, her brother.

She started in our very first day as transfer students at Franklin High. It could only have been Peggy those girls in the lunchroom were imitating. According to them, this is the way it went.

"Present, Mrs Oates," she had answered when the teacher had called out her name. And the *way* she said it. You would have thought she was acting on a stage. Every eye was on her. I could just picture her sitting as stiff as she could at her desk, her eyes straight ahead, as if she were too grand to look at anyone.

And the way she was dressed that day—the way she always *tries* to dress—like a fashion model! Most of the students wore sweatshirts and sandals. No wonder she made everyone so uncomfortable.

Then on the third or fourth day of school I overheard her talking to a couple of girls. "Well, it was a last-minute decision. Mother and Father didn't really want to move away, but Father knows how important he is to the company, so he agreed to come to Lewisville to help out . . ."

Darn right, Mother and Father didn't want to come to Lewisville. Dad had a nice job back in Bakersfield. But his company had already laid off a lot of people, and Dad had to go where they sent him or get laid off like the rest.

That was only the beginning. Peggy really laid it on those girls.

"Our new terrace is not nearly large enough," she said. *Terrace!* Why we hardly have a front porch. And then she told them we never ate dinner before *eight*. Heck, we always eat at six, like everyone else, unless Mom forgets to unfreeze the chops, which happens once in a while. But nothing can be ordinary for Peggy. Why, she'll never call anything by its regular name if she can use a French word instead. Where does she get her ideas?

We've got pretty nice parents—plain, but solid. It was sure tough on them to leave Bakersfield after living there for 30 years. But I must admit, Peggy didn't make it any easier on them. How she complained. "I can't leave all my friends behind." Who was she kidding? Peggy couldn't really call a single person in Bakersfield her friend.

And did she give my folks fits when they were looking for a new place here in town! My parents have never really had much money. Anyway, they would never think of spending more money than they should just to impress people. Naturally, Peggy pestered them to get one of those huge apartments in the new high rise on Denton Place. You can imagine how much a three-bedroom apartment costs in that building!

She finally had to settle for the house we found on Market Street. It's a nice little place. And I don't mind if I have to sleep on a sofa bed in the living room. Did Peggy make a fuss about that, though: "Mother, you can't be serious about taking this place. If Arnie sleeps in the living room, where will I entertain my friends?" Her *friends!*

But things have a way of catching up with people. And Peggy eventually got herself into a bind. It happened when she finally met a boy she thought was good enough for her. His name is Tom, and he is new in town too. I was sitting close enough to hear bits and pieces of what she was telling him one day outside on the school lawn. Boy, how I wish I had had a tape recorder with me!

"Father's country club friends . . ."

"The garden party . . ."

"The society page . . ."

"French Provincial furniture . . ."

She went on and on like that. I wouldn't have believed it if I hadn't heard it myself. But the best part came when Tom asked her for a date.

"I'll come over to your house tonight and pick you up. How about eight o'clock? And by the way, what's your address?" he asked.

"Oh, no, Tom. I'm not going straight home this evening. Why don't I just meet you in front of the movie?" You should have seen Peggy's face!

You think that's the end of the story? Not on your life! About 7:15 that evening I was on my street corner talking to one of my friends. And who do I see walking towards me? That's right—Tom.

"Hi, Arnie. I'm supposed to meet Peggy in front of the movie at eight, but I was running early so I thought I'd just take a chance and drop by. Is she at home?"

I tried to keep a straight face. "Oh, she's home all right."

"Which house is it?"

I almost choked with laughter as I pointed it out. I watched him go up to the door. Then he hesitated and looked back at me as if he thought I might have been pulling his leg. Finally, he rang the doorbell. As I walked toward the house, Peggy opened the door. I heard her say . . .

Annotations

bill *here: Am.* banknote – **I guess** *sl.* I suppose – **to stick up for s.o.** to defend or support s.o. – **phony** ['fəuni] *sl.* false or insincere person – **sure** *here: sl.* certainly – **transfer student** ['trænsfə(ː)] student coming from one school to another – **lunchroom** *Am.* restaurant that serves light meals – **sweatshirt** ['swetʃəːt] *Am.* T-shirt – **darn right** [dɑːn] *sl.* that's true – **to lay off** *here:* to give notice – **to lay it on** *colloq.* to exaggerate – **porch** [pɔːtʃ] roofed entrance to a building – **heck** *colloq.* mild expression of anger, surprise etc. – **mom** *colloq.* mother – **chop** small, thick slice of meat with bone in it – **to kid s.o.** *colloq.* to deceive s.o. – **folks** [fəuks] *colloq.* members of o.'s family – **to pester** to annoy, to trouble – **huge** [hjuːdʒ] very large – **high rise** *Am.* tall apartment or office building – **fuss** unnecessary worry or excitement – **into a bind** [baind] into trouble – **lawn** [lɔːn] area of grass that is looked after – **boy!** expression of pleasure, surprise etc. – **movie** ['muːvi] *Am.* film – **not on your life!** certainly not! – **to be running early** (usually of a train etc.)

to be ahead of time – **to drop by** to visit s.o. – **to choke** to be unable to breathe because of s.th. in the throat – **to pulls s.o.'s leg** to say untrue things to s.o. as a joke

Questions on the story

1. What does Arnie mean when he says that Peggy 'can act like a $3.00 bill'?
2. How did she behave on their first day at Franklin High?
3. How was she dressed? How were the other students dressed?
4. Why did the family come to Lewisville, according to Peggy? Why did they really come?
5. What sort of place would Peggy have liked to live in?
6. Why did she make a fuss about the house her parents chose?
7. What does she tell Tom about her family and home?
8. What does she say when Tom suggests picking her up that evening?
9. Why does Tom come to her house anyway?
10. Why does he hesitate before ringing the doorbell?

What happens now?

1. When Peggy sees Tom at the door, she has two choices:
   a) She can go on lying to try and get out of this situation.
   b) She can admit to Tom that she lied.
   Which alternative do you think she will take, and why? What might Tom's reaction be in either case?
2. Now complete the story, as told by Arnie:
   'As I walked toward the house, Peggy opened the door. I heard her say . . .'

Just Like Your Sister

Audrey knew this would be the most important day of her life. But would it be the beginning of a new and better life, or . . . She didn't dare finish her thought.

The face of the kitchen clock was so stained from the leaks in the ceiling that Audrey could hardly make out the time. Six o'clock—still an hour and a half before she would be able to make her phone call. For the hundredth time that day, she searched her sweater pocket for the piece of paper with the number. It was still there.

Audrey's mother was at the stove preparing supper. Suddenly, she turned around and said sharply, "Audrey, don't just sit there doing nothing! The devil finds work for idle hands. Have you finished your homework?"

Audrey was shaken out of her thoughts. "Yes, ma'am," she dragged out the words. She didn't like lying to her mother. "But what was the point of studying?" she thought. By this time tomorrow evening, she would probably be miles and miles away from this house and everything she hated about it.

Once again, she reached into her pocket. Then she stood up nervously and walked into the next room. Maybe Baby was awake. How nice it would be to play with her one more time. But no, Baby was sound asleep.

Back in the kitchen, she checked the clock again. Only 6:10. How slowly time was was moving. Her mother was still busy at the stove. Soon the usual supper of cabbage and turnip greens with pork fat would be steaming on the table. "How did that woman always have so much energy after a long day's work," Audrey wondered.

"The good Lord meant that we should have one big meal a day," her mother often said. And somehow, "the Lord" always provided it, whether money was scarce or not.

"Well," her mother said as she turned to her, "how about setting the table."

Audrey obeyed silently. Out came the cracked, chipped dishes from the cupboard, the patched, worn tablecloth from the drawer. How depressing they were. How depressing it was to be so poor.

Suddenly, Audrey noticed an unopened letter on the cupboard

shelf. It was addressed to her mother. By looking at the handwriting, she knew it was from Bernardine. Across the front of the envelope her mother had written "Return to sender."

Audrey finished setting the table and sat down, but her heart was beating quickly. She wanted so much to say something about the letter, but she didn't dare. Her mother would only say, "The Lord never meant that girl to be my daughter!" She'd be angry at Audrey for bringing the subject up.

It had been nearly three years since she'd last seen her sister. How she missed her, and how much she needed her at times.

"You'd better feed Baby now." Her mother handed her a bowl of hot cereal. "I'm running late, and I want to be on time for prayer meeting."

Audrey felt like yelling at the top of her voice: "Stop calling her Baby. Give her a name. She's Bernardine's baby and she's almost three years old."

Audrey entered the tiny room with the cereal in her hand. She looked around. How happy she was going to be to get out of this place. Those few broken sticks of furniture. That narrow bed she used to share with her mother *and* Bernardine. She'd never live crowded like this again, she vowed to herself.

Baby awoke and started laughing. She was always glad to see Audrey. She was such a strange child. She never cried. Audrey bent over her and hugged her tenderly.

"Baby's the wage of sin," Audrey's mother often said, "or else she would've talked by now. The Lord knows what He's doing when He gives us our cross to bear."

It was true that Baby couldn't talk. And she hadn't yet learned to walk, either. But Baby was good, and she was so lovable . . . Tears came to Audrey's eyes as she lifted a spoonful of cereal to Baby's mouth. She would miss her terribly when she left. Who would care for her and love her the way she did?

Poor Baby hadn't had a very good start. Audrey began thinking about Baby and Bernardine. Four years earlier Bernardine had run away from home with a man she hardly knew. A year later she came back looking thin, tired, and kind of old. The man had wandered off and left her with a tiny baby.

But Bernardine didn't stay at home very long. One day she just disappeared again. No one knew where she had gone. A neighbor said that Bernardine had run off with another man and was living in a nearby town. Another said that he had seen her in a nightclub with some pretty fast company. And there were other stories . . .

"If Bernardine has sent a letter, she must be in real trouble," Audrey thought to herself. "Maybe I ought to open it myself and . . ." She heard the oven door slam. Supper was ready. Audrey gave Baby her last spoonful and hurried into the kitchen. Six thirty-five, the clock showed. Another 55 minutes.

Audrey's mother was already sitting at the table. Her head was bowed. She was ready to say the blessing. Audrey dropped down into her chair and lowered her eyes. Her mother was "running late" but she had to give a full five minutes to the Lord. When Audrey finally heard, "Thank You Lord for all You have given us," she sighed with relief. She would have liked to have said, "That's a laugh!" They ate in silence. When they were finished, Audrey's mother said another blessing. She always said one before and after every meal. "Thanks before and thanks after!" Audrey sneered to herself. "And thanks for what? For misery and silence?"

Audrey cleared the table and began to wash the dishes in the cracked sink. A roach ran across the wall in front of her. No matter how clean her mother kept the place, there were always roaches. "Only another 25 minutes," she whispered to herself as she glanced at the clock.

Her mother came back into the room in her only good dress. "Tonight I'll be coming home later than usual," she said. "I promised Sister Mary I'd give her a hand with some things." She left without another word.

"Good!" thought Audrey, "that will give me enough time . . ." She went over the whole thing in her mind. At seven-thirty, she was to call Martin at his hotel. He'd tell her where to meet him, and they'd decide where to go from there.

"Don't bring anything with you, Babe. I'll get you anything you need," Martin had said. "Thank goodness he'd said that," thought Audrey. She had nothing to bring.

Audrey had to keep telling herself she was doing the right thing. Martin had been very kind to her, and he made her feel important. He treated her like a full-grown woman. But she really hadn't known him very long. Was she going to make the same mistake Bernardine had made?

"No," she said to herself. "It isn't the same thing at all. I can take care of myself." Deep down, Audrey felt that any kind of life would be better than the one she had.

It was now twenty minutes past seven. Still ten minutes to go. She'd walk down to the hall phone now. She wanted to make sure no one would be using it.

But just as she was about to step out into the hall, she heard an unfamiliar noise coming from the apartment. It was Baby. And she was crying—crying for the first time! Audrey ran back into Baby's room and took the child in her arms. "Why is she crying? Does she understand that I'm leaving?" Audrey asked herself.

"Don't worry, honey," she began to soothe Baby. "I'll be back for you, I promise. I won't let you stay here. I'll get some money and take you to the best doctor in . . ." Baby stopped crying. Audrey put her back into her crib. Audrey realized with a start that it must be seven-thirty.

She rushed out the door and down the three flights of stairs to the telephone.

No one was there. She put her dime in the slot, took the paper out of her pocket, and dialed the number carefully. The moment had come!

Her hand was shaking. Six, seven, eight rings. Finally, she heard a voice. "Hotel Albin."

Still out of breath, Audrey could hardly get out the words: "Could I . . . speak to Mr . . . Martin Johnson, please?" Her throat felt dry and tight.

She waited. Her heart was pounding. Then she heard the voice say, "I'm sorry. Mr Johnson checked out of the hotel about noon today."

"He . . . what?" Audrey cried out in disbelief. But the only reply she heard was a click as the phone was hung up on the other end.

For a while she stood there, too shaken to move. Tears streamed down her face. Finally she started up the rickety old staircase. Each step was torture. Would she never, never get away from these smelly hallways?

At the top of the stairs, she realized that Baby was crying again. Audrey ran in and took her up in her arms. "Don't cry . . . I won't be leaving after all," she sobbed. And she pressed her cheek against the child's until their tears mingled.

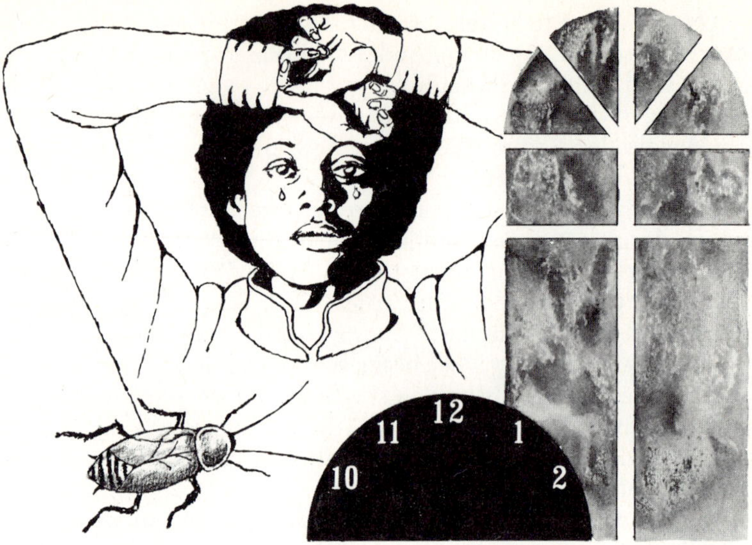

After a while, Baby quieted down. She seemed to be smiling. "I'll always be with you," Audrey whispered. Then she tucked Baby into her crib and walked quietly out of the room.

In the kitchen she broke down completely. Never had she felt so desperate before. For a moment she thought of running down the stairs into the streets—running and running until . . . But where would she run to? Martin had been her only hope. Now he'd let her down. He was no better than the man who had ruined her sister! Maybe her mother was right. Maybe all men are rotten. It was a good thing she had found out now . . . But Martin . . . He had seemed so different . . .

Suddenly, Audrey realized that there were footsteps on the stairs. Slow footsteps. She held her breath. The sound stopped just outside her door.

Was her mother back from prayer meeting so soon? Was a neighbor coming to pay a call?

There was a light knock at the door. Then, two ideas flashed across Audrey's mind, one after the other: It might be . . . Martin. Or it might even be . . . Bernardine!

A second knock. Louder this time. Baby started to cry again. Audrey hurried over to the door and opened it. She let out a startled cry as her heart skipped a beat. There standing before her was . . .

Annotations

leak [liːk] crack or hole which allows a liquid or gas to escape – **ceiling** [ˈsiːliŋ] upper surface of a room – **sweater** [ˈswetə] pullover or woollen jacket – **stove** [stəuv] *here:* electric or gas cooker – **to drag out** *here:* to say slowly and with difficulty – **sound asleep** fast asleep – **cabbage** [ˈkæbidʒ] green, leafy vegetable – **turnip** [ˈtəːnip] root vegetable – **to chip** to break a piece off – **to patch** to put a small piece of material over a hole etc. – **cereal** [ˈsiəriəl] any kind of grain used for food – **to be running late** (usually of a train etc.) to be behind time – **to yell** to shout – **stick of furniture** roughly made piece of furniture – **to vow** [vau] to promise – **to hug** to hold tightly in the arms – **sin** breaking of God's laws – **kind of** *sl.* to some extent – **fast** *here:* taking part in pleasures that some people think are wrong – **oven** [ˈʌvn] closed-in space which is heated to cook food – **to slam** to shut noisily – **to sneer** to show by o.'s expression that one has no respect for s.o. or s.th. – **roach** =cockroach: large, brown insect sometimes found in kitchens – **to glance** to give a quick look – **babe** [beib] *colloq.* term of familiar address to a woman – **thank goodness** milder form for 'thank God' – **honey** *colloq.* darling – **to soothe** [suːð] to make (a person) quiet or calm – **with a start** with a shock – **out the door** *Am.* out of the door – **dime** American coin worth 10 cents – **slot** opening in a machine for a coin to be put in – **to dial** [ˈdaiəl] to form the number of another telephone – **to pound** to beat violently – **to check out** to pay the bill and leave – **to hang up** *here:* to end a telephone conversation – **rickety** [ˈrikiti] likely to collapse – **to sob** to draw in o.'s breath while crying – **to mingle** to mix – **to tuck s.o. in** to pull the bedclothes up around s.o. – **crib** baby's bed – **desperate** [ˈdespərit] filled with despair – **to let s.o. down** to disappoint or fail to help s.o. – **rotten** [ˈrɔtn] bad – **to pay a call** to visit – **to skip** to miss

Questions on the story

1. Why is Audrey waiting for 7:30 to come?
2. Who is the unopened letter from?
3. Where is Audrey's mother going that evening?

4. Who is 'Baby'?
5. How does Audrey feel towards Baby?
6. What has happened to Audrey's sister?
7. What sort of person is Audrey's mother?
8. What happens at 7:30?
9. Why does Audrey feel so desperate?
10. What does she think when she hears a knock at the door?

What happens now?

1. Who is at the door? If it is Bernardine, what will the mother's reaction be when she gets back? If it is Martin, will Audrey run away with him and leave Baby?
2. Write two possible endings to the story:
   'She let out a startled cry as her heart skipped a beat. There standing before her was . . .'

Honor Thy Father and Thy Mother

"No. Sorry. I can't leave now. Who knows what they'll be like when they get back here."

"But Tony," insisted the voice on the other end of the phone, "these people from State College are announcing their decision this afternoon. They'll probably want to talk to you. They'll probably want to see you act again. This might be your only chance for . . ."

"I know all that, Ross. And I appreciate your calling . . ." Tony's voice could not hide the bitterness he felt. That drama scholarship meant the world to him. Of course, his parents hadn't saved any money to send him to college, and he probably wouldn't be able to go without a scholarship. "There'll be other years, Ross. I'll just have to wait a while, that's all."

"Oh, don't give me that, Tony. Who do you think you're kidding? If I had to put up with a father and mother like yours . . . It isn't fair to you!"

"That's enough, Ross! My parents are having a rough time. They do the best they can. Anyway, I won't have you talking about them that way."

"OK, fella, it's your problem—but I hate to see your future going down the drain because . . ."

"That's not your affair, Ross. I'll be seeing you." Tony quickly hung up the receiver. He felt he had to do something—throw the telephone across the room, yell, slam a door, anything. Why couldn't anyone understand?

Sure his parents were hard to take. But they *were* his parents, and he *did* care about them. There had been times when he could talk to them. But now they were . . .

But he didn't want to say it, not even to himself. Anyway, there were the kids to think of. He had to stop all this feeling sorry for himself. Lynn and Willie would be marching in soon, hungry as ever. They'd be expecting their dinner on the table whether Mother was back or not.

Just then, the front door flew open and Lynn burst in, shouting, "We're starving." She walked into the kitchen, followed by Willie. Tony knew what she'd say next.

"That lunch you made us was for the birds. We're getting awfully tired of jelly sandwiches. That was the third time this week . . ."

Tony tried to look cheerful. "Yeah, but I gave you two different kinds of jelly. Don't say that isn't something different."

"Oh, some joke. Why don't you go on TV?"

"Sure," Willie added, "and then we'll have enough money for *three* kinds of jelly." It wasn't really funny, but they laughed anyway. They enjoyed being silly together, though their jokes wouldn't make sense to anyone else.

Tony, Lynn, and Willie had shared many moments like these, especially in the last year. They didn't have much else in their lives.

Tony felt more like a parent than a big brother. He did the best he could to keep them happy. But sometimes it wasn't easy. Whenever he'd arrange for them to do something special, one of the kids would always ask, "Can we all do it together?"

"Uh, uh," Tony would say, "Dad's got to work late," or "Mom's got some extra shopping to do . . ."

The children weren't fooled. Sometimes they got mad and sometimes they were hurt, but on the whole, they accepted things. And they trusted Tony to keep things going.

Tony looked up at the kitchen clock. Five-thirty. Mom and Dad should be home any minute now. But what if it was going to be one of those nights they didn't come home at all?

"Let's give them another 15 minutes," he said to the kids, who were already seated at the table. "Come on—get rid of those long faces. You won't starve to death in 15 minutes."

Tony hurried to the stove. He couldn't let the soup boil over this time. To keep busy, he stirred the spaghetti sauce once again. His hands were tense. "What's it going to be like tonight?" he kept asking himself. "Oh, please God, let everything be all right tonight."

"Five forty-five. No use," he thought out loud. "OK, kids, let's eat," he called to them. "Hey, Willie, wash up! You know better than that."

The soup tasted pretty good, even if he did say so himself. But Tony had had lots of cooking practice. Willie was soon reaching for a second bowlful. Then they heard the sound of loud, angry voices coming from the hallway. The three dropped their spoons and looked at one another. They knew now what kind of evening it would turn out to be.

"Go on. It was your fault. I didn't break the stuff," their mother was now shouting across the living room. "If you wouldn't have opened your mouth to him, he wouldn't have thrown us out . . ."

"He had no right . . . I was gonna pay for the mess," their father yelled back at her.

The noise of their argument continued for a few moments, then stopped suddenly.

"Oh, hello, sweeties!" Tony's mother now stood smiling at the kitchen door. Her hair and clothes were messy looking, her makeup was all smeared. "How are my babies?" She leaned over Willie first and planted a wet kiss on his cheek. Then she stumbled over to Lynn and kissed her too. Lynn had wanted to turn her face away. The smell of whiskey made her sick. But she couldn't hurt her mother's feelings.

"And how's our Tony tonight?" their Dad asked in a big, cheery voice.

"*Our* Tony! Was that supposed to make up for their being late? For their acting this way?" Tony asked himself bitterly.

"Oh, it's dinner time already," said Mom. "Goodness, how I lose track of time . . . Thanks for getting things started, Tony. I'll go get the . . ."

"No, Mother, you don't need to . . ." Tony said. But she was already rattling among the things on the kitchen counter. In a minute, she returned, empty-handed. "I'm so sorry. I can't seem to find the . . ." Suddenly, she had to catch hold of the table to support herself. "I'm a little dizzy," she said with a weak laugh.

"It's OK, Mother, I'll manage . . ." But no. She was back at the stove. For a moment, Tony turned around to see what had happened to his father. There he was, already sprawled on the living room sofa. He'd probably sleep it off there till morning.

Crash! All three jumped up from their chairs. The spaghetti lay in messy globs all over the kitchen floor! "Oh dear," their mother began to wail, "I can't do anything any more."

Tony quickly found the mop and began to clean up the mess. The children just stood in the middle of the floor, too shaken to move. All they could do was stare at their mother. She was stomping around in the gooey mess, crying louder and louder, the way alcohol always made her cry.

Finally she said, "I'm just no good tonight. I'm going to bed. I'll get out of your way. I'll be all right later. I'm so sorry, children . . ." Somehow, she managed to make her way up the stairs.

Willie looked at Tony. Then he ran out of the house. Lynn put her head down on the table and began crying. Tony looked around him at the mess in the kitchen and began to feel more and more hopeless. The poor kids—to have to see this, night after night. Would it never change? No, it was only going to get worse.

"Hey fella!" Tony looked up. It was Ross, standing in the kitchen doorway. "You did it! You got the scholarship!"

For a moment, he couldn't believe his ears. "You gotta be kidding."

"Kidding! They were so impressed that they awarded you a scholarship without a second audition."

Tony let go. "Wowee!"

"They even arranged for your train fare. The new term starts early at State, and you've got to be there by the end of the month. Mr Jones, the college representative, will be here soon with all the forms for you to sign. Isn't that the greatest thing . . ."

Another crash—this time from upstairs—followed by a loud curse. Ross knew it could only be Tony's mother.

Ross began looking all about him. Sticky spaghetti was spilled all over the floor. Lynn, her head on the table, was crying her eyes out.

And in the living room, Tony's father, snoring and gurgling, had slipped half-way off the sofa onto the floor. "Oh, no!" Ross gasped.

"There! Now you see for yourself why I can't go."

"Can't go? Are you crazy? Tony, what are you doing to yourself?" Ross began to plead. "Are you going to spend the rest of your days baby-sitting for your brother and sister and playing nursemaid to two drunken parents? You've got your own life to live. You've just got to get away from here. State's giving you the chance. Please, Tony, tell Mr Jones 'yes' when he comes."

Tony didn't answer. The room was very quiet, except for his mother's grumbling upstairs. Tony looked at his father—then at Lynn.

Just then, the doorbell rang. They knew who it must be, but no one made a move to answer the door. The bell rang again. Ross walked to the door and opened it. There stood Mr Jones. He slowly took in the scene around him.

Tony looked up and said, " . . .

Annotations

thy [ðai] old form of 'your' – **to appreciate** [əˈpriːʃieit] to be thankful for s.th. **scholarship** [ˈskɔləʃip] sum of money paid to a student so that he can study – **don't give me that** don't try and make me believe s.th. that isn't true – **who do you think you're kidding?** you can't fool me – **I won't have you talking** I won't let you talk – **fella** *sl.* fellow – **drain** pipe or channel for carrying away water etc. – **to hang up the receiver** to put back the part of the telephone that is held to the ear – **to yell** to shout – **to slam** to shut noisily – **hard to take** hard to bear – **kid** *colloq.* child or young person – **starving** very hungry – **for the birds** *sl.* not good – **yeah** [jɛə] *sl.* yes – **silly** foolish – **uh, uh** [ˈʌˈʌ] *sl.* no – **dad** *colloq.* father – **mom** *colloq.* mother – **stove** *here:* electric or gas cooker – **tense** *here:* strained to stiffness – **to wash up** *here: Am.* to have a wash – **gonna** *sl.* going to – **mess** state of dirt, disorder or confusion – **sweetie** [ˈswiːti] *colloq.* term of affection – **makeup** [ˈ– –] – **to smear** to spread and make a mark – **to stumble over** to walk in an unsteady way – **I'll go get** *sl.* I'll go and get – **to rattle** to make a number of short, sharp sounds – **dizzy** having the feeling that everything is turning round – **to sprawl** [sprɔːl] to sit or lie with the arms and legs stretched out – **to sleep it off** to recover from s.th. (*here:* the effects of alcohol) by sleeping – **glob** *Am.* round lump – **to wail** to cry or complain in a high, loud voice – **mop** long pole with cloth or other material at the end, used for cleaning floors etc. – **to stare** [stɛə] to look for a long time with wide-open eyes – **to stomp** *colloq.* to stamp – **gooey** [ˈguːi] *colloq.* sticky – **you gotta be kidding** *sl.* you must be joking – **audition** [ɔːˈdiʃən] test for an actor before he is given a part in a play etc. – **to let go** *here:* to show o.'s feelings – **wowee!** [ˈwauˈwiː] expression of pleasure, excitement etc. – **fare** [fɛə] money charged for a journey by train, bus etc. – **to spill** to fall or cause to fall out of s.th. – **to snore** [snɔː] to breathe noisily while sleeping – **to gurgle** [ˈgəːgl] – **to gasp** [gɑːsp] *here:* to catch o.'s breath in surprise – **crazy** *sl.* mad – **to plead** to beg – **to grumble** to complain

Questions on the story

1. Why does Tony say he can't leave the house?
2. What chance is he probably missing?
3. What is, in fact, wrong with his parents?
4. What sort of relationship does Tony have with Lynn and Willie?
5. How do the parents act when they arrive home?
6. How do Lynn and Willie react?
7. Who arrives then? What does he tell Tony?
8. What is Tony's first reaction to the news?
9. What does he say when he has had time to think?
10. Who arrives at the end? Why has he come?

What happens now?

1. If Tony decides to leave home, what do you think his parents' reaction will be? What will happen to Lynn and Willie?
2. Tony has probably asked himself these questions, too. What decision do you think he will come to, and why?
3. Now complete the story as you think it will end:
   'Tony looked up and said, "..."'